ASTRONOMICAL SURGERY

FEEL THE THRILL

ANIKET BHOWMICK

This book is dedicated to many of the people who are facing this kind of issues due to the World war between Germany and Many other allied and axis country.

It is written so that every person should know that even child has many problems in their life by which they are unable to focus on their life. Even though there are lots of other problems, this kind of problems which are shown here are rare but still gives moral support. It has lots of suspense as a person can actually face in their life. But every person gets the chance to find out those answers.

Contents

FOREWORD

This book is made for the personal preview of the charecters shown here. This is an imaginative charecter story but hence it would happen with me, you and all the readers. This type of condition has not taken place ever with me but every child has lots of problems hence many of them quit. This story shows how to fight with our problems and reduces possiblities to quit the life. It has many confusing parts but still there are interfaces where i was bit confused to complete the story. I was advised by many people to write more things about real life.

Preface

The author chose to write about this topic as he has faced different kind of problems and also relating to those conditions, he still fought in his life. No one should quit their life hence this story was being written by the author. There were many other topics which the author might use but he found about the people who are still suffering in this Russia-Ukraine war. There were many culprits in Germany-Russia war which are shown in the book. There are several genre of the book as author tried to make it more intresting that would make the reader more interactive with the story.

I

STRAGEGIC SUCCESS

Introduction: Milli Mellate was one of the youngest cyclist trainers who entertained many of the worldwide news communication which was telecasted a year ago. Which was the first day when you succeeded to your goals? Talking an inspiration from Serena Auñón, a Russian astronomer; Milli Mellate was 14 and thought to be an astronomer. His mother Maria Antoinette Mellate was a young entrepreneur who sells food from home online through some resources and claims some of money for home.

1984

1. When Maria was pregnant, she wished to have a daughter but his husband Mr. John Mellate wanted a son. Maria was unable to give birth to a baby. Due to some health issues, she was unable to give a healthy baby. The baby was handicapped and when they came to know about it, John decided to quit the baby and kill it before birth. Due to this reasons, Maria and John fought and after some months, they divorced. Maria wanted to get divorced with John before pregnancy She knew that John won't ever accept an abnormal baby and planned.

2. In 1982, they were married but were not happy with this marriage. After marriage, they were forced to have a baby from their parents; Maria did not ever accept a baby with him. So, she just planned to make a copy of baby's health report when her baby was tested during pregnancy. As of report, baby was abnormal and its some of the parts can't work or missing from the body.

3. The report was totally fake as she knew that after watching to the report, he will give up the baby. She was quite confident that her plan will succeed. Her plan succeeded somewhat, because John said to give up the baby. Her plan was not full proof. When John enquired to his colleagues and doctors, he came to know that majority of times, the report is incorrect.

4. This made him to be forced that the report is incorrect and accepted the baby to born. Maria's plan was failing and she just lose the confidence and thought to have a baby with John itself. After three days, John saw the original report in Maria's bag. He did not react on it; he was confirming that which report is original one. Then he came to know that Maria has planned to get divorced.

5. She was curl out of the brain about the situation. John knew the whole plan but he did not fight with Maria. Without thinking on any situation, he requested his lawyer friend to send the divorce notice directly to Maria without any discussion. His friend has suggested not to get divorced because Maria alone might not be able to handle the upcoming baby.

6. He denied to the suggestion and finally sent the divorce notice. Lawyer said that John has to send money to Maria for the baby's development. He agreed to send money.

7. When Maria came to know about those papers, she just found herself guilty and happy too that after failing her plan, she succeeded. She found herself guilty because John is his real father, both father and mother has right on the baby. But she wanted the baby alone which made themselves to get divorced. Her strategy failed but instead she succeeded for her goal.

Sticking to the Goal

8. Mille was weird about his parent's condition and he knew that his father is already died before his death. John went to his school and saw the black out of the luck in the notice board. The hand written copy was about an international cycle race, his friends challenged him not to participate in this race. He denied to accept the challenge but his friends disheartened him. He went to his home and thought about it for the whole day. After a long conception to the challenge, he still has retracted to deny the cycle race championship. But when he slept, his conscious mind started interfering in his dreams which made him realize to participate in the cycle race.

9. Hence, he was forbidden from the challenge, he still wants to deny the challenge but nevertheless getting stuck to his goal, he finally agreed. He practised and practised to ride the bicycle as fast as possible. Before a day of the cycle race, the school was kept in maintenance of electronic appliance. The maintenance team regrated to the school that there are no faults in any of the appliance but, at the night before the international cycle championship. It was dark room where air conditioner was forgotten to shut while maintenance was taking place.

The air conditioner, due to cold temperature and shot circuit has busted. A fire broke out in the school and the guard was the first to be witnessed about the fire. It made the championship to be cancelled or to be delayed for some time.

10. John was quite sad about to be happy on the sight after hearing news. Every news channel had witnessed some different reasons to increase their view point but as the guard was the eye witness, his confession made the fire, a big political issue. Fortunately, there was no loss of life in the fire broke out. After a month of the incident, a Maria came to know that her father-in-law was a Nazi (supporter of Hitler). They came to know that they were not safe at all as her father-in-law was a Nazi, hence Germany was defeated. But as they already divorced, they have less fear in their mind. There were many provisions where were faced on those days by the Russians but still John had made a friend named Kerstif. Maybe the divorce was due to this reason too. Russians were not harmed more but still they were in risk due to John. Kerstif might change there life.

Bloody Night

11. When John was 19, he felt in fondness with a German girl, Kerstif Daljon. She was the relative belonging to the family of Adolf Hitler. John did not know about it. He partly spent his most of the time with her and shared every family detail to her.

12. A fond of darkness in his house when he returned from his college was noticed by him. It was 5.30 P.M. when the sun was ready to set. He was knocking the door and speaking to his mother as shouting tone "Открой дверь". There was no reply from inside. He thought that there was something wrong there so finally he started hitting the door and finally the door opened.

13. A dark room where everything was destructed on the sight and Stalin was missing. He was nervous and heart beat was high. He then went to the room and found her mother hanging. She was found suicided without any note. He was nonetheless shocked nevertheless depressed about the situation. He immediately called police on the spot of incident.

14. Due to the elections, the police were said to report themselves in such places so they were unable to be present on the suicide spot. The body of Stalin remained at that place itself hanging for about 11 hours. At such situation, john had gone blank and was unconscious and deadly living at that part of time when he saw her mother in such condition.

15. When the police came, they investigated and came to an extension that there is no such evidence that it was a murder. John believed by seeing the bad condition of room, that it was surely a planned murder. "The last reply to me before some minutes of suicide, the time of calling was none of the stressed sound tone." Said the police in the confession media and publication.

16. This made some misplacement in the suicide case, as if a person commits or want to commit suicide; the voice of the person might be depressed or somewhat stressed. But it was not as psychologist replied to the case.

17. None of the evidence was up to the mark if she has really committed suicide or murder. As John was mostly unconscious and unable to speak a word, his confession was the necessary one to close or to continue the case. This case became a political issue in Russia and sooner had taken place in many destructions and anxious condition to the public. John did not wake up for 3 days, then he was consulted by a doctor (a physiatrist). He said after some health check that he was in comma due to the shock.

18. The public made it hilarious because their concern was the police has not reported at the suicide spot as john has called them. Yet they had not taken any action on the criminal and a serious injustice. Police confessed to the print and electronic media that they were busy in the protection of electoral places. The excuses were not ignored and the Moscow police department was culprit according to the public.

19. The closest friend of john was Kerstif Daljon, who cannot be ignored in this case. As she was non-resident of Russia and also a member of nazi. The Russian people doubted her because of such evidence of 2nd world war. Stalin was already in the fear that she was husband of a nazi was explained by her brother who was far abroad in France. They haven't also contacted but knew everything *happening there. When her passports were sent in verification as if she was a German or not. They found that it was an American passport which was issued from Yerba Buena (now San Francisco).*

20. A question arises that if she is an American then why she was heading her identity as German as nazi and relative of Hitler?

21. She was kept in crime investigation department, Chuvashia bureau for several days. John was in comma, so he cannot confess any important thing. Kerstif yet said that if she is a German girl and the American passports are because she lived in America for several years. But yet the full truth was missing. She was torched and beaten by police yet she has not said the whole.

22. She was doubted the most at the point of suicide but then after about half a month of suicide, john finally wake up and confessed a couple of things. His revelation made the case close and the matter was not in hand of police.

Conclusion

THE QUESTION ARISES THAT WHAT HE SAID IN CONFESSION?

The confession was just shocking for all of them. John has became controversy those days but still he believed in god. He knew that something would happen which might change their life. John doubted on kerstif but still his heart did not ever felt that if Kerstif can do anything wrong with them. He confessed in front of media and public that his mother was depressed and there were many circumstances where she might suicude anytime. She was treated in many hospitals in every country and hence she suicuded. This statement closed the door to increase inspection for the case and hence the case was reported to be normal suicide and was stated to close within 3 days after completeing all the legal works.

Why did he confessed this type of statement? was he lying or speaking truth, if so then why didn't he said truth which might help him to inspect more on this case and find the actual culprit?

II

Is that the pain?

Introduction: After Stalin's shocking and unknown death, Kerstif was yet a secret character. What do you think, who is Kerstif actually? There can be several ways by which he can find his father. One of the ways are the Russian Entrance Examination which has been described in the story. We came to know about the plan of John to find the real culprit as he had already confessed and closed the case which was still in review. After the case closed, he planned to find the actual culprit in the way of Bishop's movement in a chess(chapter3). There are many new charecters and new ways by which John can find the murderer or if he was actually correct that it was real suicuide.

Hilarious public

1.

There passed two months after the death of maria, john suddenly packed off the bags and had booked the flights to Boston logan to join NASA. It switched to the year 1998 and nothing changed in the life of John. 'Less feelings or the stone-hearted person' well said by the public to John. What could be the reason that he suddenly went to NASA without outcoming the chances that what would happen then?

2.

It was supposed by the police and other investigation department that it is a suicide. Was NASA his actual goal for succeeding in his life or the plan to find the actual culprit? When he was born, he was gifted a locket by his father which was one and only gift preceded by him. That locket was given by him and he said that "cela protégera John des problémes á venir dans sa vie. Cela ne lefera pas sesentir seul!".

3.

It means that the locket can help him in problems and would not ever feel alone. Hopefully he might had not felt alone on those conditions due to that. 'All among of us' was a French comedy show which had made a humorous scene that made the whole France laugh. A boy migrated to USA after death of his mother. France would have laughed about it because the way it was said was funny and which became a trend on all social media pages.

4.

Her case after death of 2 month again came in trend with many interviews by john. Did you get that why did he migrated to USA? Without any complaint or any inquiry to the legal department well known as judicial department; his case again started with a public reaction that "justice pour maria". The doubt suddenly went to Kerstif, the public has attacked on her house.

5.

That attack changes into a war, why? Because she was related to German dynasty which was considered powerful those times. That war did not continue so long as Kerstif said to Simard Hitler to stop the war. There were lot of confusions between them. Again, John just quit on these circumstances.

6.

He 'quit' does not mean that he suicided, he quit to find the murderer as the small death was changing its shape into thousands of deaths. The love, freedom, sensation given to John by his mother was undoubtedly hilarious. He faced many problems in his life. He died very soon after the divorce but there are still many questions about his life which was questioned by Milli.

Question Hour

1.

The sacrifice of john was known by Milli as he found a diary written by Kerstif which was found by him. Still there were lots of questions in his mind about his dead father. A night passed and his questions increased about the confession given by John.

2.

He was thinking that "what if I was there that time and would help him!". He couldn't also ask to her mother directly about his father. He was told from his birth that his father is already died before his birth. Where was John? Is he alive? Why do they divorce? How was my grandfather and grandmother died? Questions arises in his mind resulting zero answers from this.

3.

A mystery is something that can't be explained, escaped, answered by anyone in this world. It can only be explained by one thing, which is mystery itself. As the day passes, the interrogation increases and milli is trying to find out those answers. You might have heard about several mysterious story in film. Did you ever find it funny?

No? But why?

4.

The pain of knowing something which is irritating us is something different. It was experienced by Milli. The humorous thing happened here was that he didn't knew that what is meant by divorce. He visited certain websites for knowing those things and was experiencing interruption in his school life due to that. Having this many issues in his life, he still fought in his life and passed the russian entrance examination.

5.

This examination was taken for giving job avaiblities to russian citizens in other countries. He has passed the exams and hence was certified to go to Germany for job. His plan just became more closer to go closer to kerstif. Even didn't knew that if kerstif was alive. But there he got a friend in his college days whose father worked in Kerstif's company. John had to face many problems still Maria divorced her, she should help her for the problem which was not fair. Well thought by john"a...a....mmmm.....I think so that my mom need to find John because its unfair for him.

6.

Just because of my birth, they both divorced, as they would have thought that if i am abnormal or maybe gender inequality", They didnt even know that if John is alive or where is he living, but still they were getting regular money from John. It meant that anyhow Milli had to find john because still they are getting money from him. Many of question arise but we came to know that one of the person who could support her husband in his hard time was one and only Maria. But she didn't helped her out from these condition.

7.

The united states of America has organised an examination all over the world for russian citizen all over world which guves a better job opportunity in Germany's best company which is owned by Kerstif Daljon. He concentrated on the examination and has cracked one of them. The second examination was held in Brussels, Belgium which was an oral examination of spellings to be pronounced. He was weak in english hence he started english classes.

Finding the culprit

There starts the way to find the culprit in

III

BISHOP WAR

Introduction: - 11 years passed, still Milli was not answered with any of the question. John was a mystery for them and Kerstif was still a question. Kerstif used to write diary about John. Again, a question arises that why was Kerstif writing about john. What's your opinion for this situation?

1995

According to Dalton's theory, atoms can never be devastated nor be fashioned. It is pertinent to every second individual in this whole world. Milli's life has changed in these years. Russian entrance examination which was held in year 1984, was given by Milli. He secured much better marks than the 82 people in his school. He splintered the scrutiny and was given proposal to go Germany for the studies. Milli did not had any interaction with Kerstif. He played a game with his mother 'the game of chess in reality'. He was studying in Germany's college where Kerstif too studied and john. It was all his game to go Germany and to know about both of them in detail. 2 years back, when he came to Germany for study purpose. He had been ragged by Panerko Stevin, a German boy and also known as dictator of that college. Now they both are friends, Milli was not born to be normal boy. What is the difference between a normal and a abnormal person? He was not abnormal, nor normal; he was a kind of boy who used his brain in different way. Ragging seems to be fun for the raggers but illegal as per the German government. These were the conversations done by Panerko and Milli:

(Scene: Milli's first day at college. Panerko sent one of his friends to call Milli for some purpose)

Panerko: Hello boy, I don't want to ask any question to you neither your name. Prove that you are brave by doing something different from others, if you will not be able to do that than you will be punished.

Milli: I am already smart and brave, why should I prove my bravery to you? Yeah, but I will not deny to your work. But before than doing that, introduce yourself.

Panerko: Do you think, I am as stupid as you are? Give your phone to me. Do you think that you will ask questions to me; and I'll answer to you?

Milli: (starts laughing) I proved my bravery. But don't you think that you are coward than me.

Panerko: Wha.... What? I can't understand that how did you proved your bravery?

Milli: (smiles and walks away from them) You will come to know very soon.

How was his bravery proved? Can you guess anything? He was not a normal child. His mobile phone was taken but they didn't effort on his shirt. He already knew that ragging is fashion of every college hence he had already planned hence he had placed a small camera in his pen. He recorded the conversation in it and sent that recording to the vice chancellor of the college. This was all his bravery by which Panerko got the punishment also he proved that how smart is he. His first day of college was something different but.......................................

It is 2 years after those conditions. In these years, he made many friends in which his best friend was Joseph Darwin, an American person. Now let's see the history of Joseph Darwin; born in New York, settles in Germany due to transfer of his father's job. Mainly they both were communicating with each other through internet because Milli was very poor in English, was able to speak French, German and Russian language. The humorous scene is that the best friends can't even communicate with each other but as the day passed, they both learned each other's language. Milli shared his whole life history with Joseph. Joseph was knowing about Kerstif as his father is still working in the place where Kerstif is owner.

The game of Chess

There starts the movement of Milli and Joseph as like as Bishop. Starlin Darwin lost his job from New York, he shifted to Germany for the job but it turned his life into the black. It was the company of Kerstif where the rules and regulations were as strict as army schools. No one in this world can know about this company as it has many confidential reasons. Once he requested to go to the office but his father denied to go. The college was starting a system to give jobs in several companies in which Kerstif's German union private limited was also there.

TO BE CONTINUED

Printed by Libri Plureos GmbH in Hamburg,
Germany